D1558597

AMERICAN HEIRLOOM BARGELLO

AMERICAN HEIRLOOM BARGELLO

Designs from Quilts, Coverlets, and Navaho Rugs

by

Millie Hines

CROWN PUBLISHERS, INC., NEW YORK

To the anonymous craftswomen who were the original creators of the works upon which these designs are based

First published January 1977

Inquiries should be addressed to Crown Publishers, Inc., One Park Avenue, New York, N.Y. 10016.

Printed in the United States of America
Published simultaneously in Canada by
General Publishing Company Limited

Design: Dennis Critchlow

Library of Congress Cataloging in Publication Data

Hines, Millie
    American heirloom bargello.

        1. Canvas embroidery.   2. Canvas embroidery
                —Patterns.   I. Title
        TT778.C3H56   1976   746.4'4   76-17881
                ISBN 0-517-52469-4
                ISBN 0-517-52470-8 pbk.

ACKNOWLEDGMENTS

I am grateful to my friends Connie Thomas, Richard Beale, and Carole Strickler for helping with the samples. My appreciation to Jonathan Holstein, Sarah Melvin, and Phyllis Haders for permission to adapt designs from quilts in their collections. Thanks to Frank Hendricks and to my editor, Brandt Aymar.

Photography by David Brittain and the author.

CONTENTS

INTRODUCTION

There is much interest today in traditional American crafts. Patchwork quilts, woven colonial coverlets, and Navaho rugs are part of this important heritage. They possess a timeless beauty of color and geometric design.

Not many people today have the time to make a quilt or weave a coverlet or rug. But everyone should have time for American Heirloom Bargello. Any of the bargello designs in this book can be made in only a few evenings. The authentic designs retain the visual impact of the original articles. It isn't necessary to be able to draw to reproduce these designs since they are based on counting. The diagrams are easy to follow. Instructions are included for beginners. Names of the original patterns, with their dates and locations, are given when possible. Some of the designs are stylized naturalistic or symbolic forms; others are pure pattern. All are well adapted to textile design, which makes possible a natural transition from sewing and weaving to bargello.

Ideas for quilt patterns came from many sources. They were traded among friends and found in magazines and newspapers. The same pattern may have been used thousands of times, but each woman employed her personal color sense to create an individual work. The quilt designs in this book are taken from actual antique quilts. These are strong geometric designs which would be effective in infinite color combinations. They have been adapted for bargello and may be reproduced exactly as shown. But do not hesitate to use your own color sense to create a one-of-a-kind piece. Hints for doing this are included in the instructions.

Weaving patterns for colonial coverlets were also widely used. Colors were limited because most of the yarn was dyed at home with natural dyes. The predominant dye was indigo blue. Yellow and brown dyes were made from flowers and leaves. Natural wool and cotton were used for white. Today there is virtually no limitation on color choice. Contrasting colors of your own choosing may be used in any of these designs.

The colors and designs used in Navaho rugs often had symbolic meanings. Natural white, gray, brown, and black sheep's fleece were used along with natural and chemical dyes.

The directions given are for squares of about twelve inches. Finished pieces of this size can be made into pillows, carrying bags, and wall hangings. There are also instructions for smaller projects.

Each American heirloom design is presented in a two-page spread. Diagrams and instructions are clear and easy to follow. Each design is shown in two full-color photos. The upper photo shows the entire 12" square design reduced in size. The lower photo shows somewhat more than a quarter of the design at a scale just slightly under actual size.

GENERAL INSTRUCTIONS

MATERIALS

The following supplies were used in the book:

D.M.C. brand tan, antique color mono canvas, No. W-13-1, 27" wide, 13 threads per inch, 14 spaces per inch

D.M.C. brand Laine tapisserie, wool tapestry yarn

No. 21 tapestry needle. These have blunt points.

Scissors.

Masking tape 1" wide

Indelible, waterproof fine-line marker—"Sharpie" by Sanford was used.

D.M.C. tapestry yarn comes in an exceptionally wide range of colors. Colors are given in the book with D.M.C. code numbers to use. The printed colors may vary slightly from the colors of the actual yarn. The amount listed with the individual designs is the number of D.M.C. skeins you will need. There are eight meters or about 8¾ yards in each skein. Persian type yarn from various companies is also very effective. It is recommended if you can find it in a sufficient number of colors. Simply take the book along to the yarn store and match the yarn to the book's colors.

Feel free to alter or completely change color schemes by substituting colors of your own choosing. The samples are based on well-planned designs, so innumerable color combinations will be effective.

Tan, antique-colored canvas is preferable to white because it does not show up as much between the stitches. The size of the canvas can be counted in two different ways. If you hold the ruler as shown in the photo the count will be 13 threads per inch. If you count spaces there will be 14 spaces per inch. If you are buying another brand of canvas, make sure you know whether they count threads or spaces to determine the size. Canvas 27" wide was used for the samples in the book. Exactly half of this 27" width is just right for the designs. Penelope canvas may also be used. When cutting the D.M.C. canvas or another brand or width, make sure that you allow at least a 13½" or 14" square for each design.

Different weights of yarn and canvas may be used, but the yarn and canvas must be in proportion. A thicker yarn would be used with a canvas having fewer threads per inch; this would make the total design larger. This must be taken into account when buying materials. Most people working in needlework stores will be willing and able to help you figure such changes.

If there is no needlework store in your area, D.M.C. yarn and canvas can be ordered directly from: LeeWards Store, Attention Mike Salak, 840 North State Street, Elgin, Illinois 60120. The D.M.C. yarn can also be ordered from Merribee Company, P.O. Box 69, Fort Worth, Texas 76101. We are not sure at this point if Merribee has this type of canvas. There are many different kinds of yarn and canvas, so make sure you specify the code numbers and size.

PREPARING THE CANVAS

After cutting the canvas, cover all edges immediately with masking tape to prevent unraveling of canvas and snagging of yarn. Use 1"-wide masking tape. Adhere half of the width of a strip to one side of the canvas edge, then bend the other half of the tape strip to adhere to the other side. The smooth selvage edge need not be covered.

The quarter markings shown in the photo correspond to the dotted lines on the individual diagrams given with each design. It is best to use a waterproof fine-line marker to make these lines. Ordinary ball-point pens and pencils are not recommended because they can stain the yarn. If you must use them, keep the marking extremely light.

To divide the canvas evenly fold in half at one edge. You do not want a fold line down the middle so crease only at the edge. Follow the center thread across the canvas with the marker. Keep the line as light as possible. Do the same thing in the crosswise direction.

THREADING THE NEEDLE

Use a size 21 blunt-point tapestry needle. Lengths of yarn from 18" to 24" are about right. Longer ones tend to tangle. To thread the needle, squeeze the yarn between thumb and forefinger letting about 1/16" of the end show. Ease the end carefully through the needle eye. This may take some practice. You may find it easier if the yarn is freshly cut or if you twist the end before squeezing.

BEGINNING THE STITCHES

Only one kind of stitch, the satin stitch, is used for all designs. This is used in both the straight and oblique (diagonal) versions. Although permanent knots are never used, a waste knot is used as shown to anchor the yarn to the front of the bare canvas. This will later be cut away after stitches have covered and anchored the yarn end. Hold the canvas so the selvage edge will be parallel to the stitch rows when possible because the canvas is somewhat stronger when used this way. This means it is best to put the selvage on either the bottom or top except for designs 9 and 21, where it can be on the side. To make the stitches the correct length, count the number of canvas *threads* the stitch will cover. The enlarged photo shows a stitch six threads long; this is the most common length used in the book.

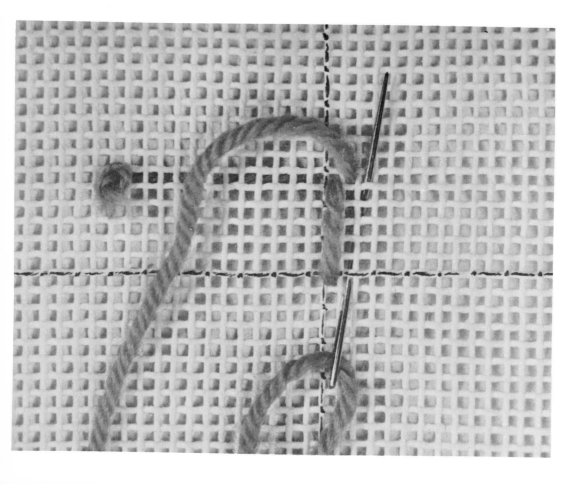

OPTIONAL CANVAS MARKINGS

Bargello is normally done by counting as you make the stitches rather than by filling in a drawing on the canvas as for needlepoint.

For some of the designs you may find it helpful to mark a grid on the canvas threads. This gets the counting over all at once. If you intend to mark the canvas, check the individual diagrams first, because a few of the designs do not fit this grid. Most of the designs are based on blocks of six stitches which are six canvas threads long. Mark every sixth thread for this system, which is shown in the photo. There does not seem to be a marker that is totally waterproof on the canvas. However, you should never wet or wash your bargello piece. The "Sharpie" seems to be pretty good. If you are using another brand do a test on a small area. Let the ink set for a few minutes, then see if it rubs off on the yarn; make a row of stitches about 2" long. Hold a steam iron over the back to make sure ink does not run. Keep the marks very light, just strong enough to see. *Count carefully.* Do not use a pencil or ordinary ballpoint pen here. Do not mark diagonal lines on the canvas. The grid shown here can be used for any of the designs that have a diagram drawn on ¼" graph paper. You may feel that these additional markings are more helpful for some designs than for others.

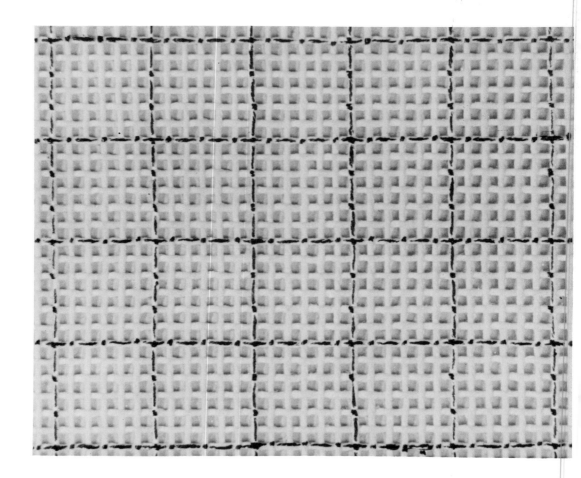

FOLLOWING THE DIAGRAMS

A small arrow is used here and in all the individual diagrams to show where to bring up the first strand of yarn. The photo shows a block of six stitches, six canvas threads long in relation to the optional marking lines. The yarn in all the black and white photos is thinner than normal to enable you to see the stitches more clearly. Your stitches will have a more bouncy and full look.

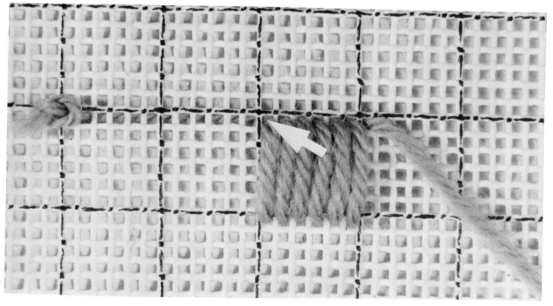

Important: *Do not pull the yarn too tight while stitching. Make the stitches with a relaxed, easy, and even tension.*

Two sizes of graph blocks are used in the individual diagrams. In the first system the individual diagram shows the entire design reduced in size. Each graph block which is a little less than ¼" represents a block of six stitches, six canvas threads long. In the shaded six-stitch block of figure 1, the arrow shows where to bring up the first yarn strand.

In the second system, a quarter of the design is shown within the dotted line close to finished size. Each graph block stands for one canvas thread and a row of blocks stands for one stitch. In the shaded six-stitch block of figure 2, the arrow shows where to bring up the first yarn strand.

Fig. 1

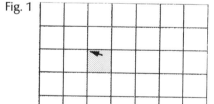

Fig. 2

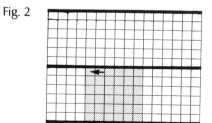

BEGINNING AND ENDING THE YARN STRANDS

These three photos show the back of the canvas.

End the yarn on the back of a bare canvas by locking it under a thread.

Anchor a new yarn strand to the work by running it through the yarn on the back of the canvas. Going right through the yarn, and not just under it, gives extra hold. It is a good idea to pinch the part with the new yarn end to keep it from pulling out while making the first one or two stitches.

End the yarn by putting the needle through the previous row of stitches on the back of the canvas.

Beginning and ending the yarn strands in the same direction as the row you are stitching makes for a smoother appearance on front.

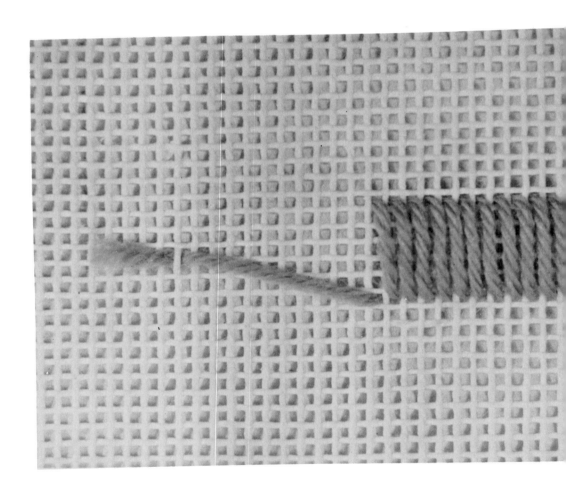

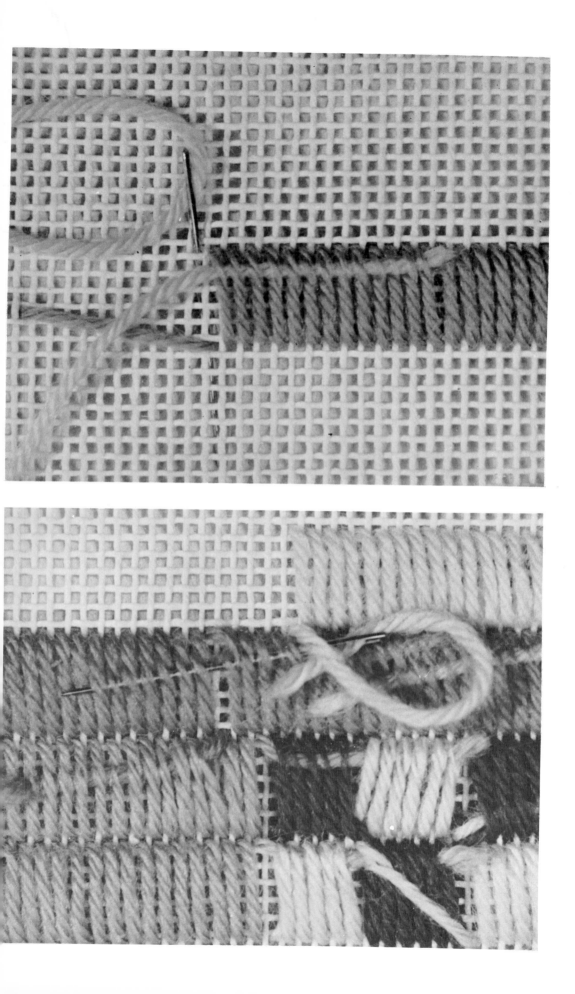

STITCHING HINTS

Hold the canvas in whatever position seems most comfortable. It is usually easiest to start in the middle of a canvas and work out to the edges. When working in the middle you may find it more comfortable to roll part of the canvas and hold it in your free hand. On some designs it is best to finish each quarter separately. When doing this, it is usually easiest to work the bottom quarter with the canvas turned around. On some designs, such as the stars and diamonds, the design is worked out and around from the middle in a spiral motion turning the canvas as you go.

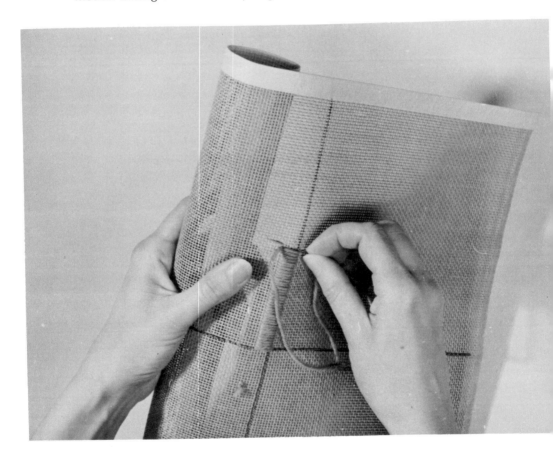

Remember not to pull the yarn too tight. Try to stitch with a relaxed and even tension. The canvas should not pull out of shape at all as it does sometimes with needlepoint stitches. After a few stitches the yarn may become more tightly twisted or the strands may begin to separate. When this happens, hold the canvas upside down to let the needle and yarn hang free and spin to normalize the yarn. This may have to be done quite often.

STRAIGHT STITCHES

Spaces in the canvas are shared with previous rows of stitches so that all canvas threads are covered. Bring the yarn strand up in an empty space and down into a shared space. The new yarn strand was added at the end of the row by bringing it vertically through the yarn on the back. Where ends of rows meet bare canvas, end yarn strands in the same way by bringing them down vertically through the stitches on the back in the rows below. Remember that the yarn used in all the black and white photos is thinner than normal to show detail. Your stitches will have a fuller look.

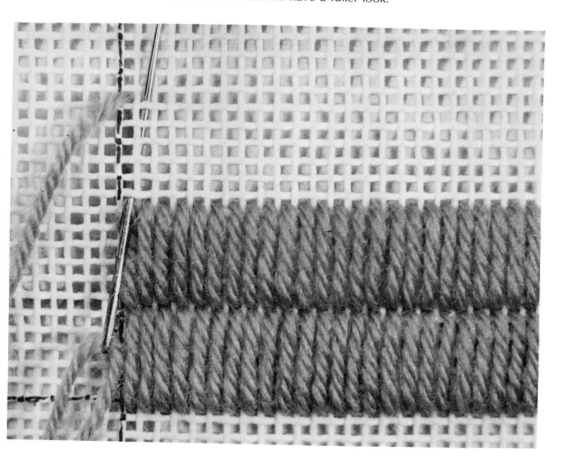

OBLIQUE STITCHES

Oblique stitches are represented on the diagrams by diagonal lines. Most oblique stitches are seven threads long as shown here. Baby blocks and pineapple have stitches eight threads long. Be sure to make the stitches shorter when you come to the border line.

PERPENDICULAR STITCHES

It is important not to leave canvas threads exposed in a finished piece. In some designs stitches are worked in both horizontal and vertical directions. These meet in shared spaces as shown. If the vertical yarn thread has been put in first, put in the horizontal row by going carefully into the spaces under the vertical yarn. This technique should be used for side borders.

TRIANGLES

Triangles are easier to understand if you look at the way they are made up from a combination of diagonal half and square blocks. Figures 3 and 4 are enlarged versions of the ¼" graph used in the individual diagrams. The numbers show the number of stitches in each section. Notice that the diagonal blocks break up into sections of five and six stitches. Notice the way the five- and six-stitch diagonal sections reverse in figure 4.

Fig. 3

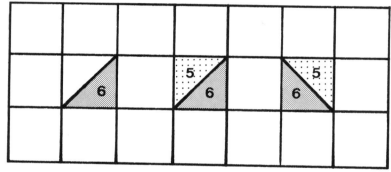

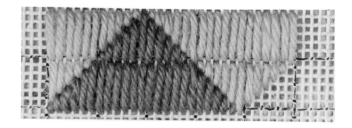

Fig. 4

DIAMOND CENTER

The center of two diamond designs is given here in steps to show how the stitches overlap. Notice that the first stitch of each group is seven threads long.

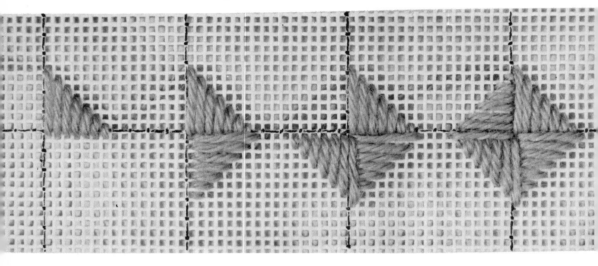

STAR CENTER

The center of the three star designs is shown here in steps. Notice that each stitch is seven threads long. The small one-thread diagonal center stitch has not been put in yet here. For the maple tree the bottom two diamonds will be part of the trunk.

CHANGING COLOR SCHEMES

Do not hesitate to change the color schemes to suit your own personal taste and decor. Patchwork quilts were done in this way. Women used the same basic designs with many variations in color combinations.

If you want to work out your color scheme on paper, put a piece of tracing paper over the black and white diagram and fill in your colors with magic marker, crayons, or paints. To figure out how much yarn you need just substitute your color for the one replaced.

FINISHING

Remove the masking tape from the edges. If your canvas looks as if it may unravel or if the edge is dangerously narrow, you can go around with a machine zigzag or small straight stitch. This is more important if it is going to be made up into a bag than for other items.

Blocking should not be necessary. The piece should just be steamed. Turn it good side down and go gently over the back with a steam iron. Do not ever let the weight of the iron rest on the piece. If the piece is slightly out of shape, it can be straightened at this time.

Your American Heirloom Bargello piece is now ready to be made into a pillow, bag, album cover, framed hanging, or maybe put to some clever and original use of your own devising.

AMERICAN HEIRLOOM DESIGNS

1~

STAR

About 1910, Pennsylvania

Finished piece 11½″ square

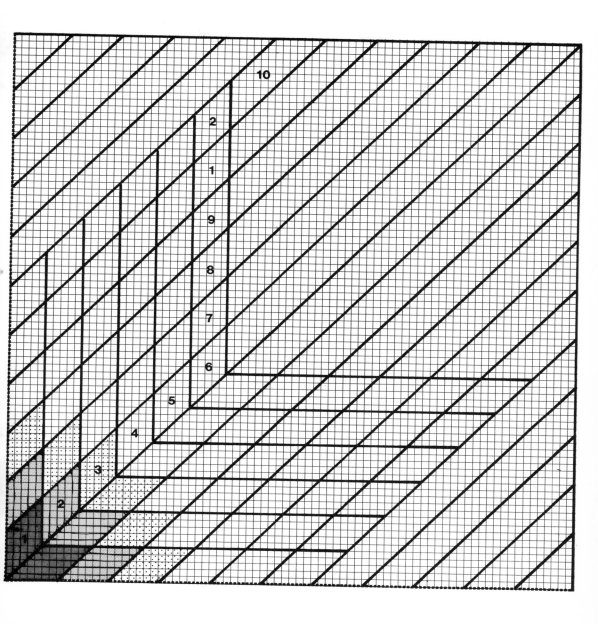

1. 7742 yellow 1
2. 7745 light yellow 1
3. 7200 pale pink 1
4. 7211 pink 1
5. 7202 dark pink 1

6. 7501 cream 1
7. 7307 navy 1
8. 7317 dark blue 1
9. 7302 blue 1
10. 7511 tan 10

Bring yarn up at arrow. Work center star composed of eight small diamonds working clockwise. Refer to star center detail on page 20. Progressively work each circle of diamonds out from center. Work star points then fill in background.

2~

SUNBURST

Patchwork quilt c. 1850

12″ square

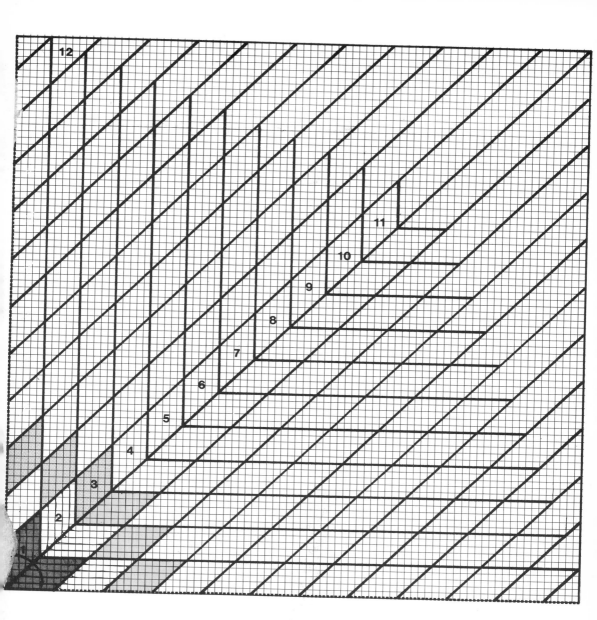

1. 7449 maroon 1
2. 7200 pale pink 1
3. 7505 gold 1
4. 7446 rust 1
5. 7439 dark orange 1
6. 7176 light rust 1

7. 7437 orange 2
8. 7435 yellow 2
9. 7431 yellow green 2
10. 7501 cream 2
11. 7549 pale green 2
12. 7511 tan 5

Bring yarn up at small arrow. Work center star composed of eight small diamonds working clockwise. Refer to star center detail on page 20. Progressively work each circle of diamonds out from center. Fill in background.

3-

MAPLE TREE

Quilt block, 1940

11½" square

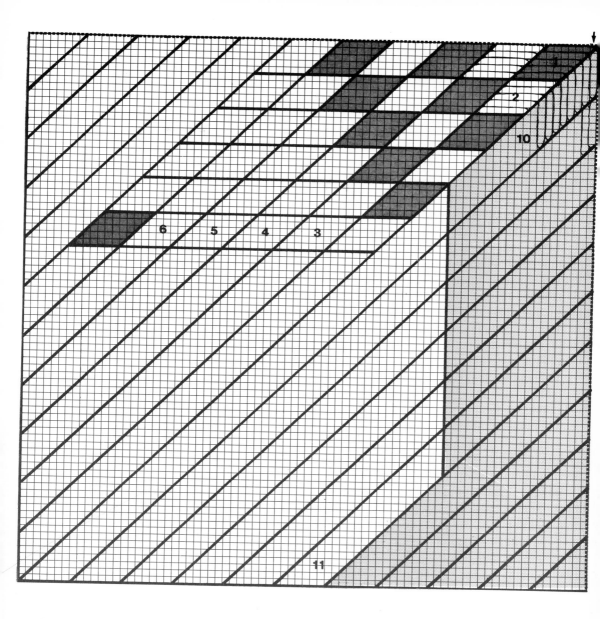

1. 7459 brown 1
2. ecru 1
3. 7760 salmon 1
4. 7850 red orange 1

5. 7205 mauve 1
6. 7606 red 1
10. 7234 gray 2
11. 7292 blue 9

Colors in branch not shown in diagram

7. 7444 gold 1
8. 7947 orange 1
9. 7437 yellow orange 1

Bring yarn up at arrow. Work small diamonds to complete large diamond-shaped section in lower left. Refer to page 20 for help with center diamond. Complete each adjacent large diamond-shaped section. The diagram of the star pattern on page 20 can be followed if necessary for the top quarters. On the alternate branch not shown, the colors from the center out are: 6, 3, 5, 7, 8, 9, 3, 4, 5, 6, 9. Work trunk, then fill in the background.

4~

PINEAPPLE

Section of a quilt, New York

12″ square

1. 7439 red orange 1
2. ecru 2
3. 7437 orange 1
4. 7489 brown 5

5. 7143 beige 4
6. 7184 rust 4
7. 7511 tan 2

In the diagram the central section is shown close to full size. Bring yarn up at arrow. Look closely at both diagram and photo to do central diamonds. Longest stitch in central diamond section is six threads long. Straight stitches are six threads long. Oblique stitches are eight threads long. Work the sections around the center, turning the canvas in a clockwise spiral. Check both color photos to finish design.

5~

POPPY

Art Deco quilt block c. 1935

12″ x 12⅛″

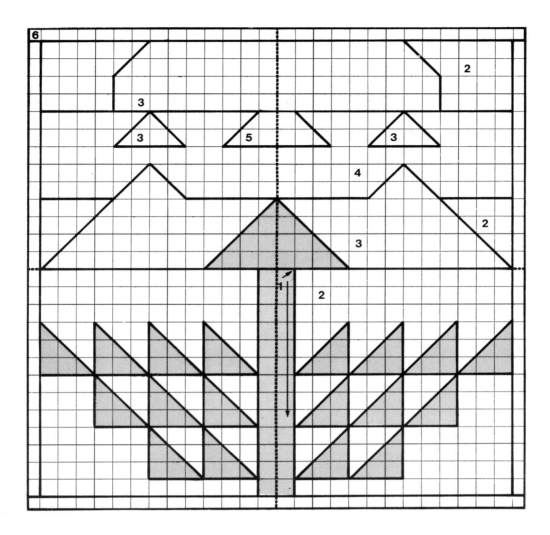

1. 7548 green 3
2. ecru 6
3. 7439 dark orange 4
4. 7437 orange 2
5. 7449 maroon 1
6. 7511 beige 2

Work stem, then flower, leaves, background, and border.

31

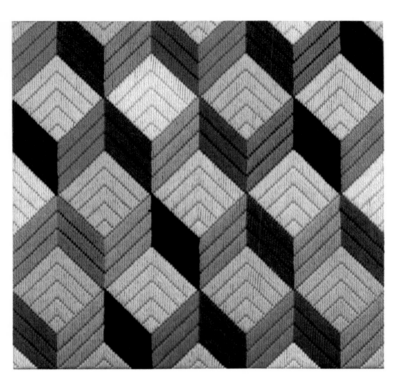

6~

BABY BLOCKS

Section of a quilt,
Pennsylvania, 1930

12" square

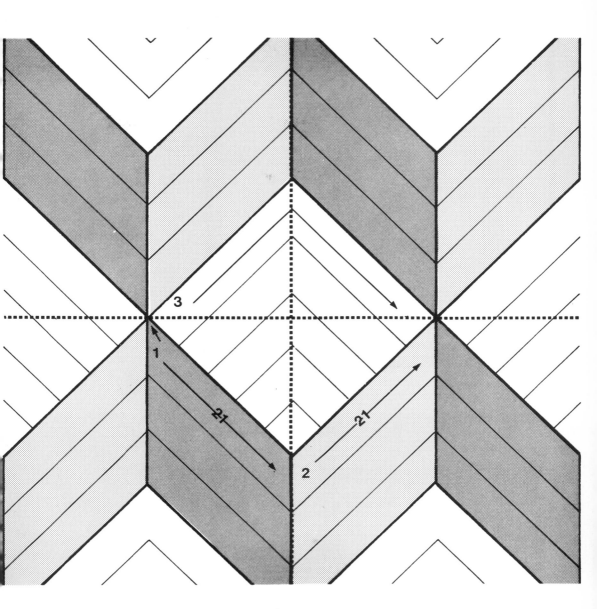

Dark Colors

7303 navy 2
7459 dark brown 2
7169 red brown 1
7446 orange brown 1

Light Colors

ecru 3
7745 yellow 1
7121 peach 2

Medium Colors

7511 tan 1
7271 gray 2
7273 dark gray 1

7439 red orange 1
7922 orange 1

Central section is shown close to full size. Each baby block is made up of a dark, medium, and light section. Any combination of colors will work well for this if you separate them into light, dark, and medium colors. Once you do the central baby blocks, the others will fall into place around them.

Bring yarn up at small arrow. Make a row of twenty-one oblique stitches each eight threads long in the dark, then in the medium, section. Notice that the first light stitch comes up two canvas threads above the second dark stitch. First light stitches are two, four, six, then eight threads long.

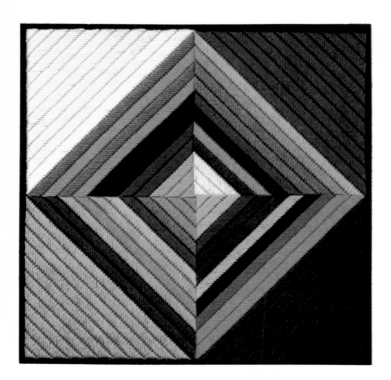

7~

DIAMOND
(variation)

1890, Kansas

12″ square

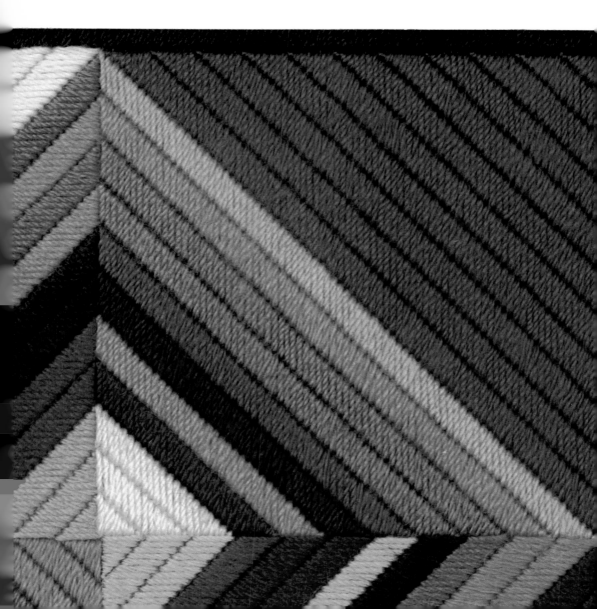

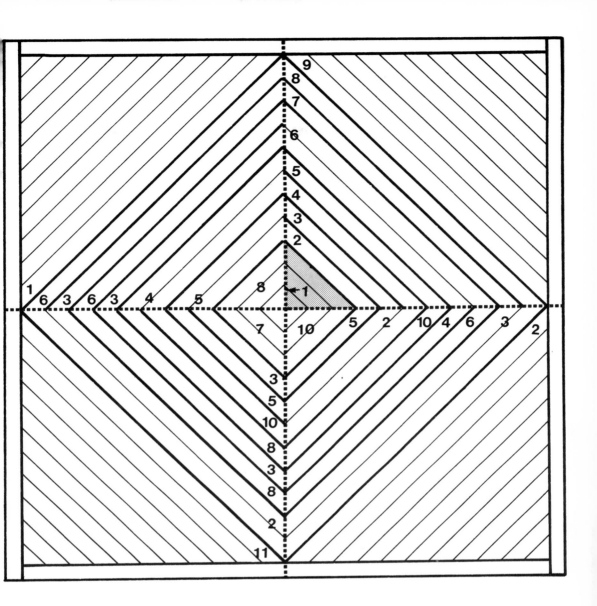

1. 7727 yellow 3
2. 7245 purple 3
3. 7708 lilac 2
4. 7449 maroon 3
5. 7169 rust 1
6. 7255 mauve 2

7. 7444 gold 1
8. 7455 wheat 1
9. 7184 rust red 2
10. 7271 gray 1
11. 7511 tan 2

Bring yarn up at arrow. Work entire upper right quarter. Refer to center detail on page 20. Turn canvas sideways to work lower right quarter. Turn canvas again to work each remaining quarter. Work border.

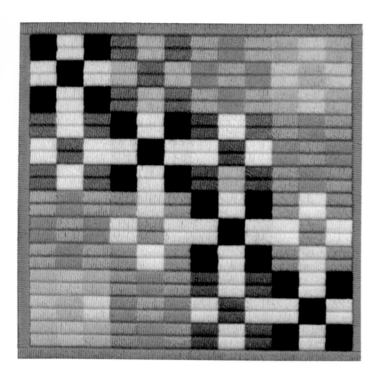

8~

NINE PATCH

Silk quilt, by Salome Lapham,
1820, Rochester, New York

11½'' x 11⅝''

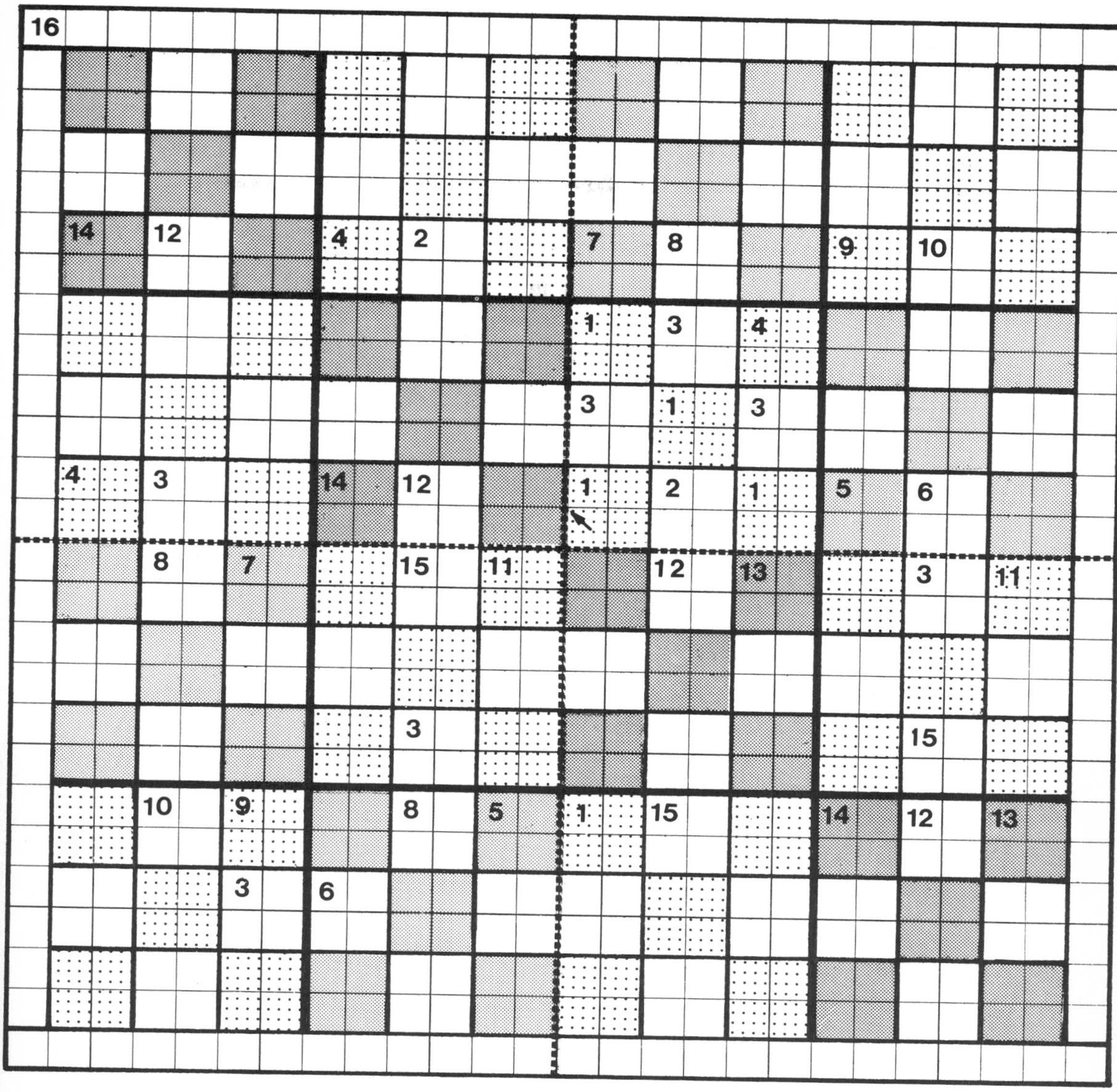
16
14
12
4
2
7
8
9
10
1
3
4
3
1
3
4
3
14
12
1
2
1
5
6
8
7
15
11
12
13
3
11
3
15
10
9
8
5
1
15
14
12
13
3
6

1. 7768 green 1
2. 7761 salmon 1
3. 7211 pink 1
4. 7547 olive 1
5. 7511 tan 1
6. 7798 blue 1
7. 7271 gray 1
8. 7313 turquoise 1
9. 7549 light lime 1
10. 7120 beige 1
11. 7548 lime 1
12. 7727 yellow 2
13. black 1
14. 7307 navy 1
15. 7200 pale pink 1
16. 7302 gray blue 3

Bring yarn up at arrow. Work each square in the nine patch blocks. Continue to do the rest of the nine patch blocks.

9~

PINE TREE

Patchwork quilt block, 1975,
Geneseo, New York

About 11½'' square

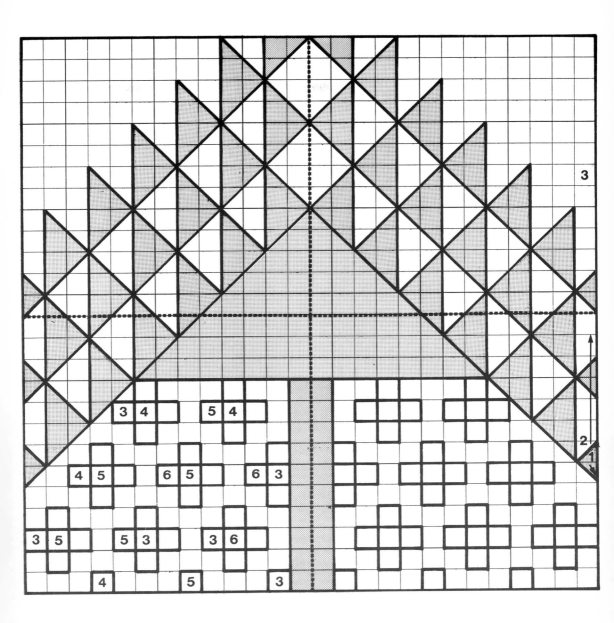

1. 7387 dark green 5
2. ecru 3
3. 7807 turquoise 4
4. 7444 brown 1
5. 7431 yellow 1
6. 7742 orange 1
7. 7912 light green 3

Have canvas selvage on side for this design. Bring yarn up at small arrow. Refer to directions for triangles on page 19. Work green triangle then adjacent white one. Continue working alternate white and green triangles. Fill in sky and base of tree. Work flowers and ground.

10~

HOUSE

Quilt block, 1942,
Pennsylvania

11″ x 11¾″

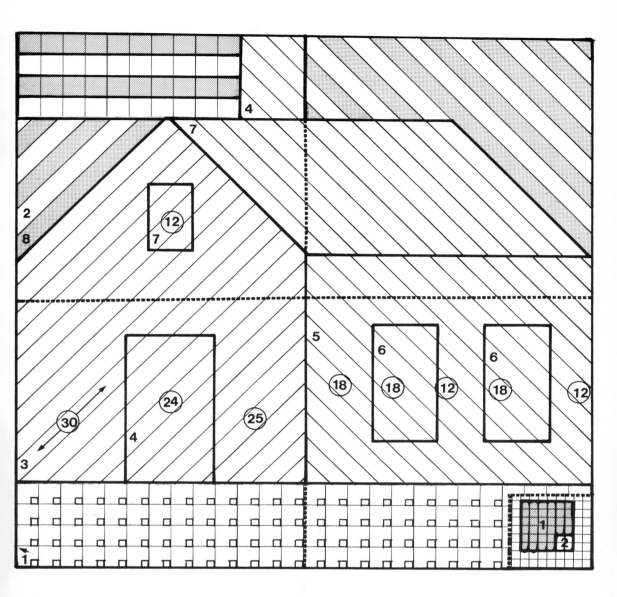

1. 7307 navy 3
2. ecru 3
3. 7727 light yellow 4
4. 7211 dusty pink 1

5. 7726 yellow 3
6. 7192 pink 1
7. 7194 dark salmon 2
8. 7301 sky blue 2

Bring yarn up at small arrow. Detail in lower right corner of diagram shows how polka dot blocks are done. Oblique stitches are seven threads long. Circled numbers give number of stitches in that row. It might be a good idea to mark the door and window rectangles in the canvas. They do not have to be exactly as shown here. The diagonal where the light yellow house front meets the roof is tricky because the rows of light yellow stitches end in two different ways in order to make a smooth diagonal line. You might be able to see this in the full-size detail.

11~

SAMPLER

Patchwork quilt, 1880,
Pennsylvania

12″ square

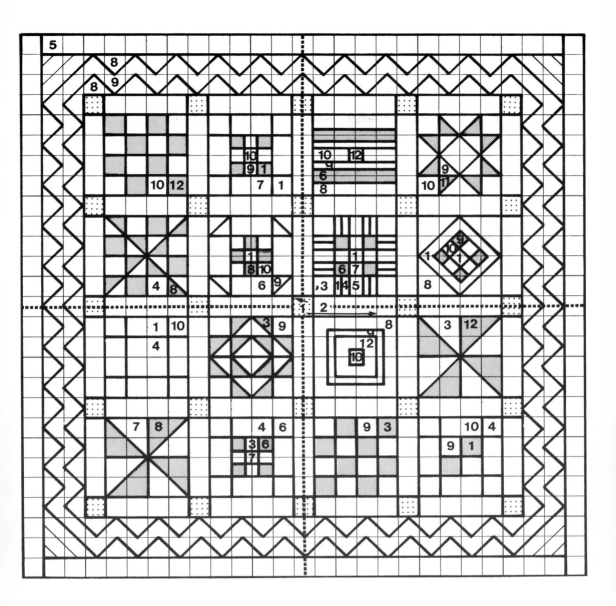

1. 7207 rose 1
2. ecru 4
3. 7313 turquoise 1
4. 7922 orange 1
5. 7141 pale pink 3
6. black 1

7. 7301 light blue 1
8. 7387 dark green 4
9. 7213 pink 3
10. 7727 yellow 1
11. 7797 royal blue 1
12. 7606 red 1

Bring yarn up at small arrow. Some of the stitches in the pattern blocks are two and four canvas threads long. Refer to photo on page 19 for triangles. Work border last. Pink oblique stitches are six threads long. The border corners are tricky. The number of pink stitches in each corner is not quite the same.

12~

LOG CABIN

Quilt blocks, silk, 1880,
New York

11½" square

1. 7946 orange 1
2. 7313 light turquoise 1
3. 7307 navy 1
4. 7243 light purple 1
5. 7301 light blue 1
6. 7241 gray lilac 1
7. 7317 turquoise 1
8. 7449 maroon 1
9. 7511 tan 1
10. 7800 sky blue 1

11. 7245 purple 1
12. 7820 dark blue 1
13. 7292 gray blue 1
14. 7797 royal blue
15. 7318 dark turquoise 1
16. 7271 gray 1
17. 7447 brown 1
18. ecru 1
19. 7200 pale pink 1

You may find the optional marking lines referred to on page 12 especially helpful for this design. Each quarter is worked separately so it is important to locate
centers accurately. Work the upper right quarter first, starting with the orange
center, bringing yarn up at arrow. Work rows of stitches around the central
square. The order in which to put in the colors is shown by the number
sequence up to 13; after that numbers begin to repeat. This is an ideal pattern
for using up odd scraps of yarn. Just separate the light and dark colors and use
the dark ones for the shaded areas.

13~

DIAMOND

Patchwork quilt, wool,
c. 1900, Amish, Lancaster
County, Pennsylvania

12" square

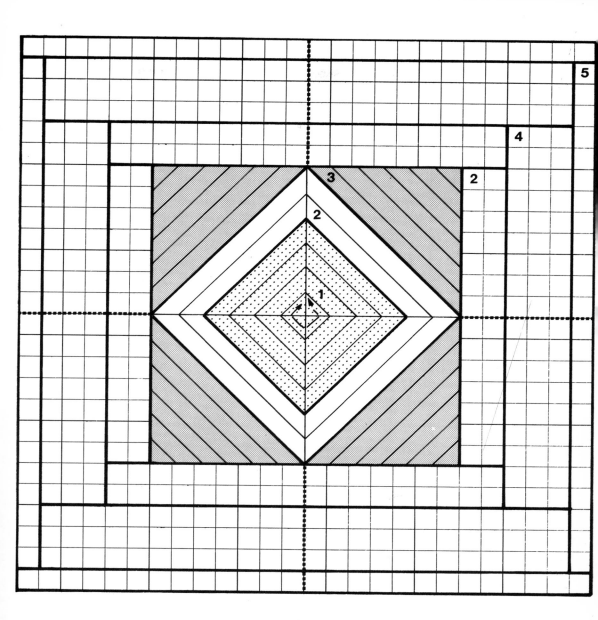

1. 7606 red 2
2. 7995 turquoise 4
3. 7797 blue 3

4. 7768 green 6
5. black 3

Bring yarn up at small arrow. Refer to center detail on page 20. Oblique stitches are seven threads long. Straight stitches are six threads long. Refer to page 18 for perpendicular stitches for border.

14~

TRIP AROUND
THE WORLD

Patchwork quilt, wool, c. 1930,
Amish, Lancaster County,
Pennsylvania

12″ square

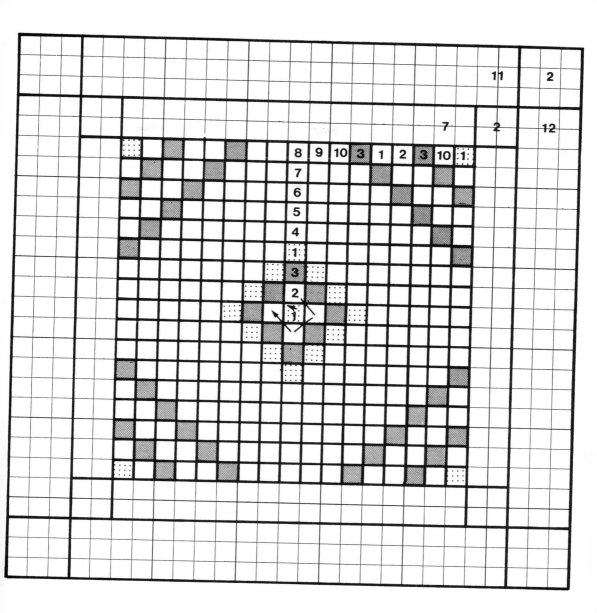

1. 7215 salmon 1
2. 7200 pale pink 2
3. 7602 rose 2
4. 7307 navy 1
5. 7241 gray blue 1
6. 7800 sky blue 1

7. 7344 bright green 4
8. 7770 olive 1
9. 7387 dark green 1
10. 7544 red 1
11. 7314 blue 3
12. 7807 turquoise 3

Begin at center square bringing yarn up at small arrow. Work each surrounding group of squares. Do border last.

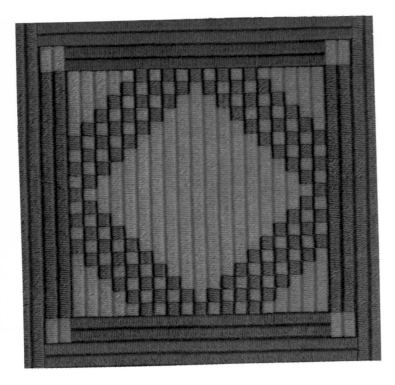

15~

TRIPLE IRISH CHAIN

Patchwork quilt, wool,
c. 1915, Amish, Lancaster
County, Pennsylvania

12" square

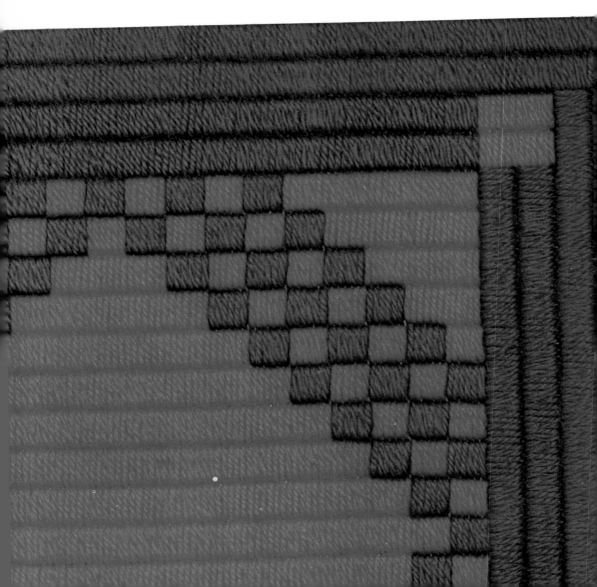

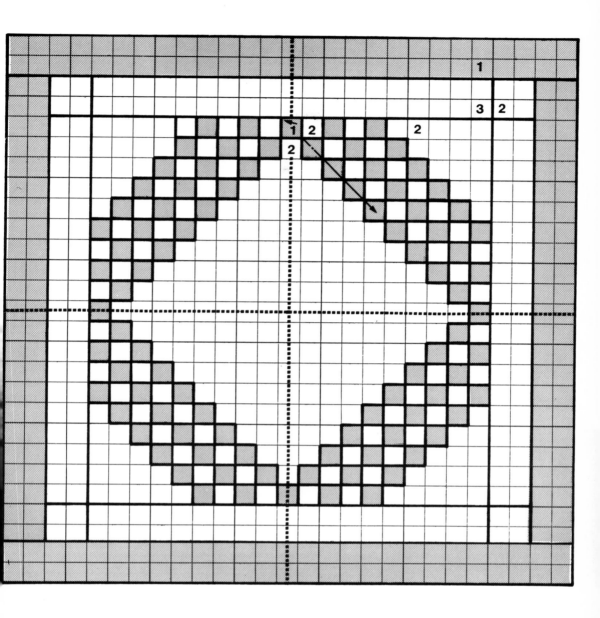

1. 7995 turquoise 7   3. 7895 lilac 4
2. 7606 red 7

Bring yarn up at arrow to begin with turquoise square. Work downward to do
diagonal row of turquoise squares. Counting carefully, continue to work entire
frame of turquoise squares around central diamond. Fill in red central diamond,
then finish red and turquoise blocks. Do border last.

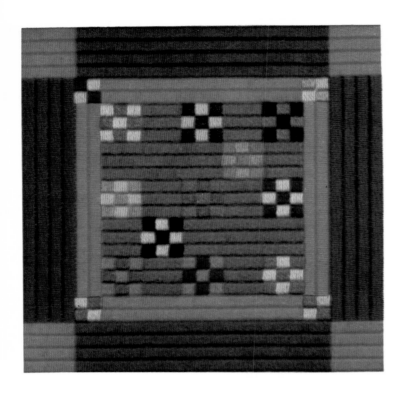

16~

NINE PATCH
(variation)

Patchwork quilt, 1900-10,
Amish, Lancaster County,
Pennsylvania

12″ square

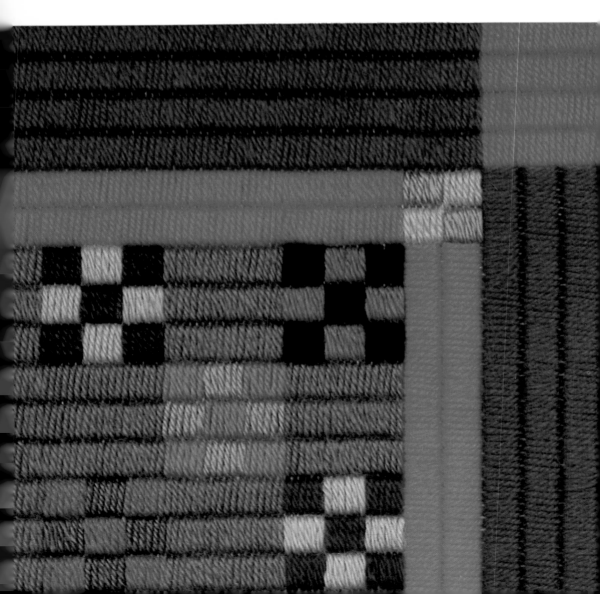

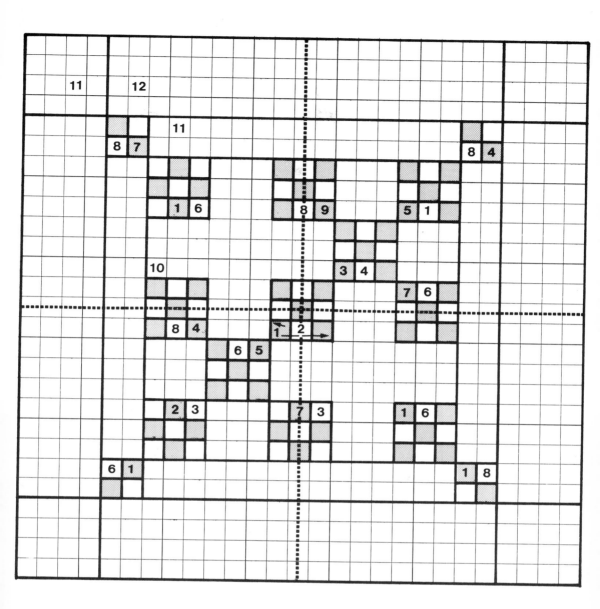

1. 7995 turquoise 1
2. 7768 green 1
3. 7439 orange 1
4. 7262 gray 1
5. black 1
6. 7211 pale pink 1

7. 7199 maroon 1
8. 7761 salmon 1
9. 7367 dark olive 1
10. 7255 lilac 3
11. 7606 red 4
12. 7169 rust 7

Begin with the center square. Complete the nine alternate color squares which make the central nine patch. Then progressively work the diagonal row of nine patches. Next begin to fill in the lilac background and complete the rest of the nine patches. Do border last.

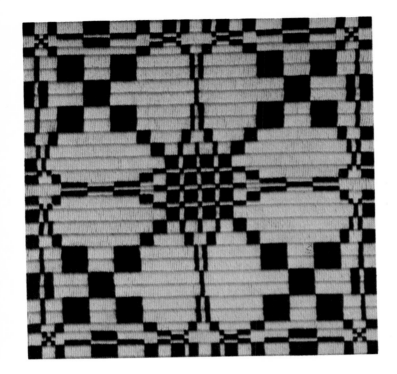

17~

ROSE PATH

Woven colonial coverlet pattern, summer-winter weave, used mainly in the eighteenth and nineteenth centuries.

11½" square

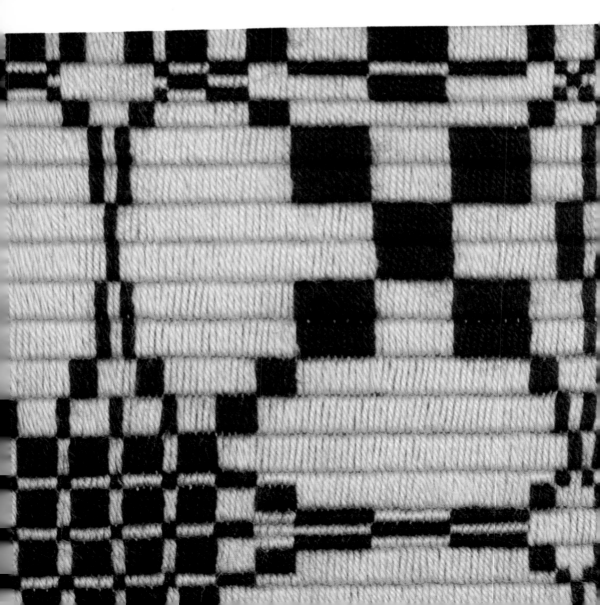

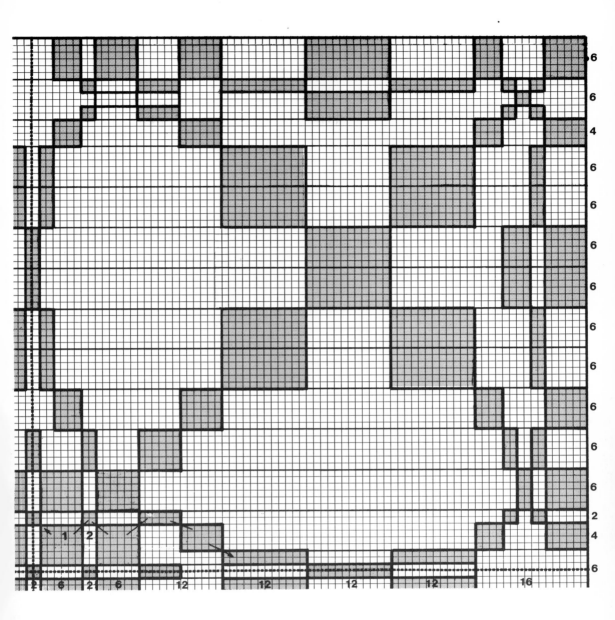

1. 7307 navy 6   2. ecru 11

Area within dotted line shows one quarter of the design close to full size. Numbers along bottom edge show number of stitches in each section. Numbers along side edge show stitch length. Start by working a horizontal row of navy stitches as shown by broken arrow. Fill in with ecru, work across rows from left to right until you come to top.

Work pattern in reverse for upper left quarter. Turn canvas around to do lower quarters. With canvas turned, lower left quarter can be followed from graph exactly like first quarter.

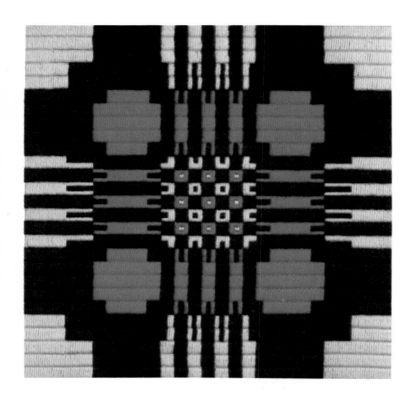

18~

DOUBLE WEAVE

Woven colonial coverlet pattern

12″ square

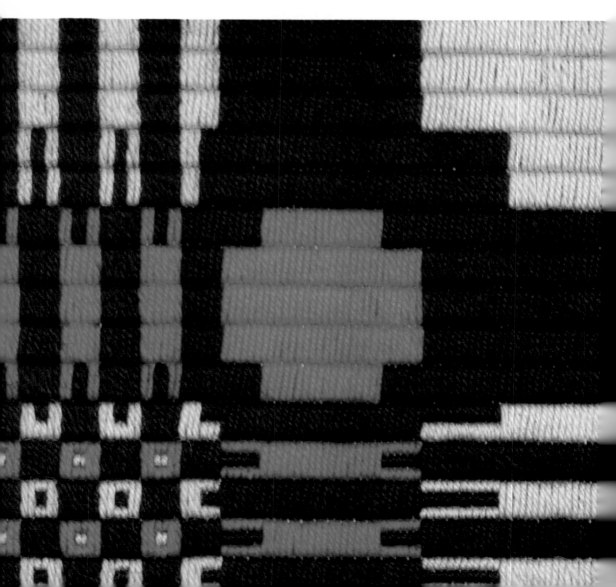

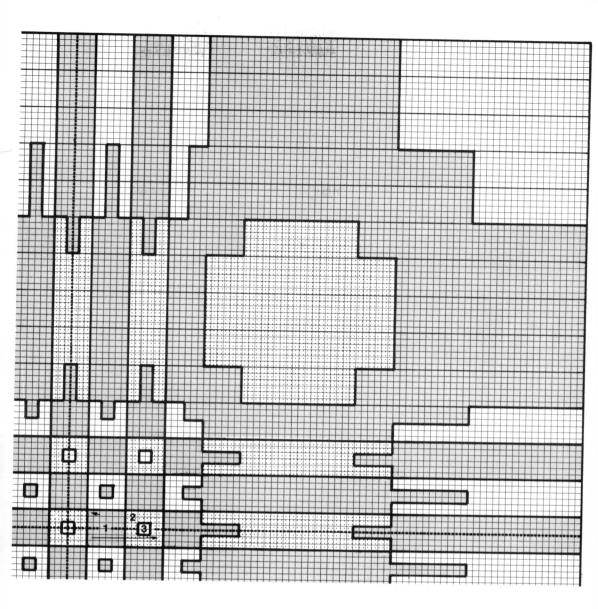

1. 7307 navy 10
2. 7544 red 4

3. ecru 4

Begin by working horizontal row of navy and red stitches. Work rows from left to right until you come to top. Work pattern in reverse for upper left quarter. With canvas turned around, lower left quarter can be followed from graph exactly like first quarter.

19~

BLOOMING LEAF

Woven colonial coverlet pattern

12" square

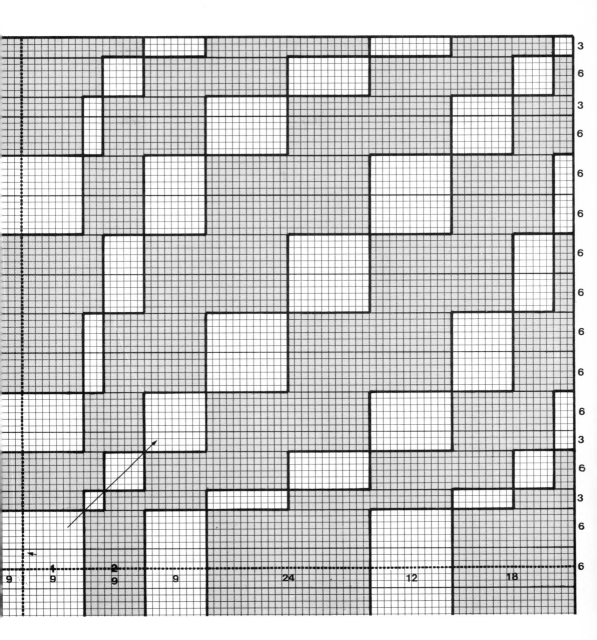

1. ecru 6   2. 7297 dark teal blue 9

For this design a faded denim shade of blue or any range of earth colors would be interesting instead of the dark blue. If you prefer a predominantly light design, substitute light for dark blocks and dark for light. Numbers along the bottom give the number of stitches. Numbers along the side edge show stitch length.

Bring yarn up at small arrow. After working the large ecru center square, work diagonal row of ecru squares. At this point it may help to draw some vertical lines to mark the edges of the blocks on the canvas. You can then either put in all the ecru blocks or work alternately between the ecru and blue.

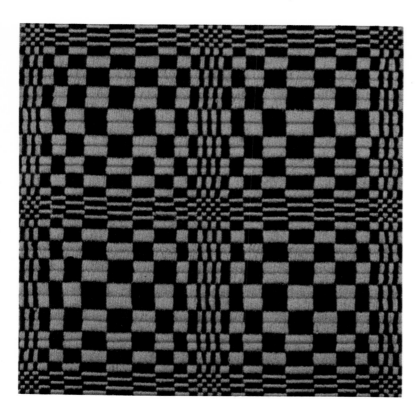

20~

CAT'S-PAW

Woven colonial coverlet pattern used mainly in the eighteenth and nineteenth centuries

12⅜″ square

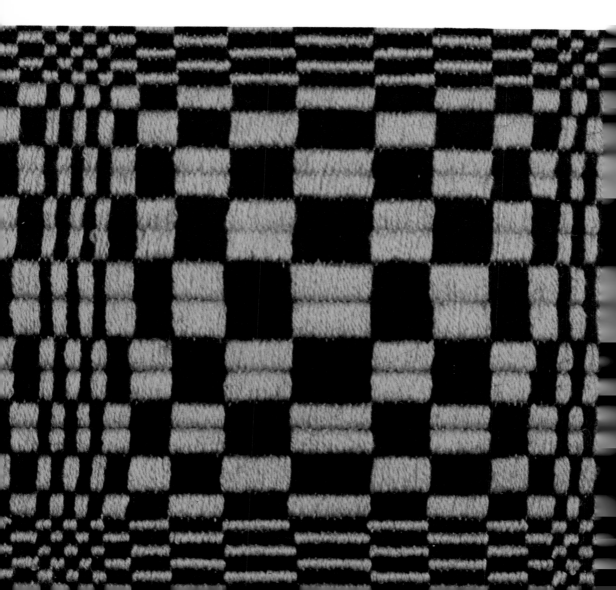

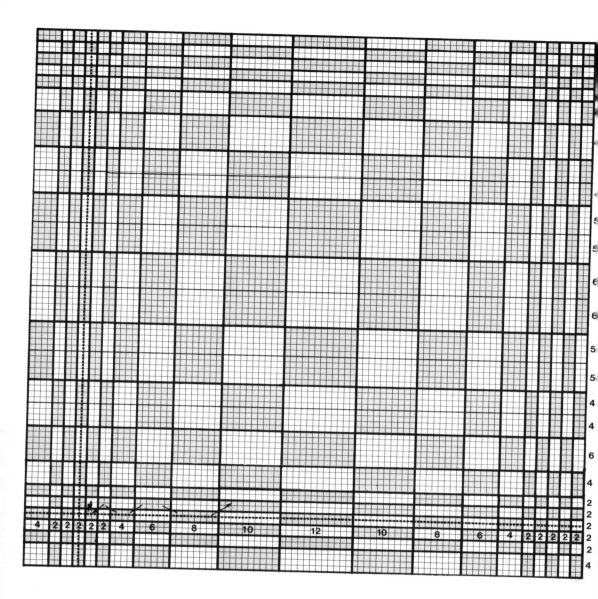

1. 7469 brown 9   2. 7677 gold 9

Shaded areas represent brown yarn. Numbers along bottom edge show numbers of stitches in each section. Numbers along side edge show stitch length. Start by working a horizontal row of brown stitches as shown by long broken arrow.

Fill in with gold. Work across rows from left to right until you come to top. Work pattern in reverse for upper left quarter. Turn canvas around to do lower quarters. With canvas turned around, lower left quarter can be followed from graph exactly like first quarter.

21~

PUEBLO BROCADING

Hopi ceremonial dance kilt,
nineteenth century

12" square

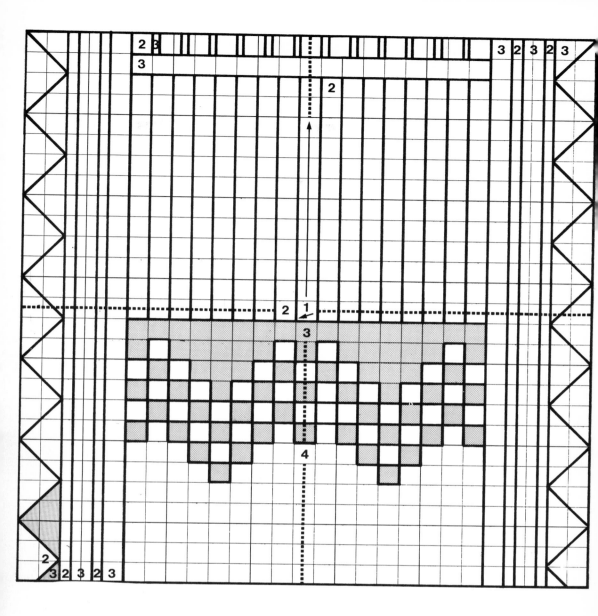

1. 7544 red 3
2. ecru 7

3. 7307 navy 6
4. 7169 rust 3

Have canvas selvage on side for this design. Begin with red and white striped area. Do navy and white blocks, then rust area. Work border last, referring to directions for triangles on page 19 if necessary.

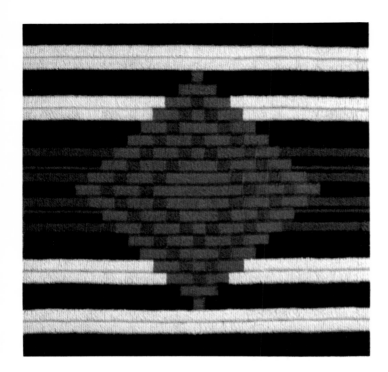

22~

CHIEF'S BLANKET

Navaho weaving, 1850-75

12″ square

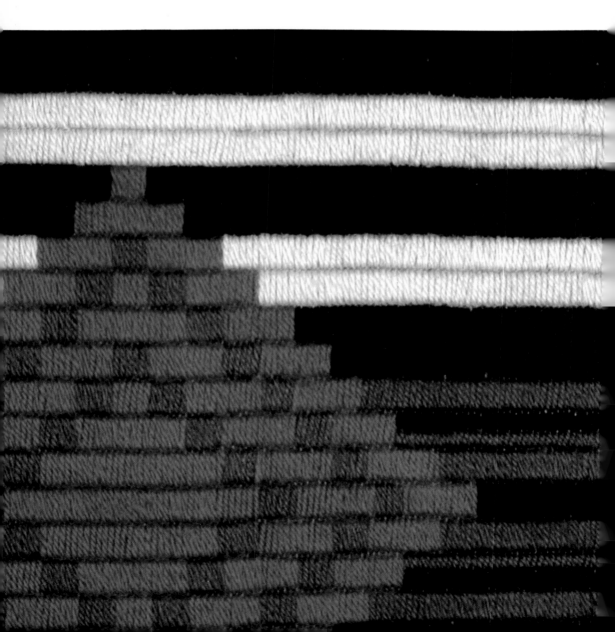

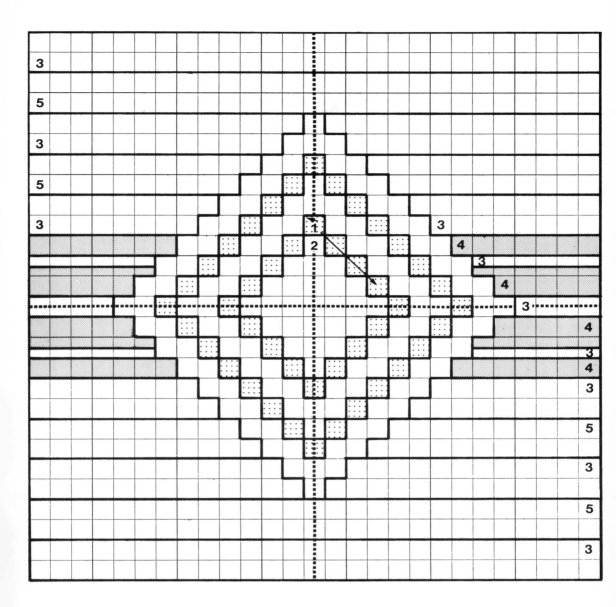

1. 7488 brown 2
2. 7184 rust 2
3. black 6

4. 7459 red brown 2
5. ecru 5

Bring yarn up at small arrow and work first brown square. Work diagonal rows of brown squares to make frame for central diamond. Fill in rust diamond, then finish rust and brown squares. Work brown, black, and white stripes. Note that some brown and black stripes are three canvas threads long.

65

23~

TWO GRAY HILLS

Navaho Rug, twentieth century

12⅜″ x 13″

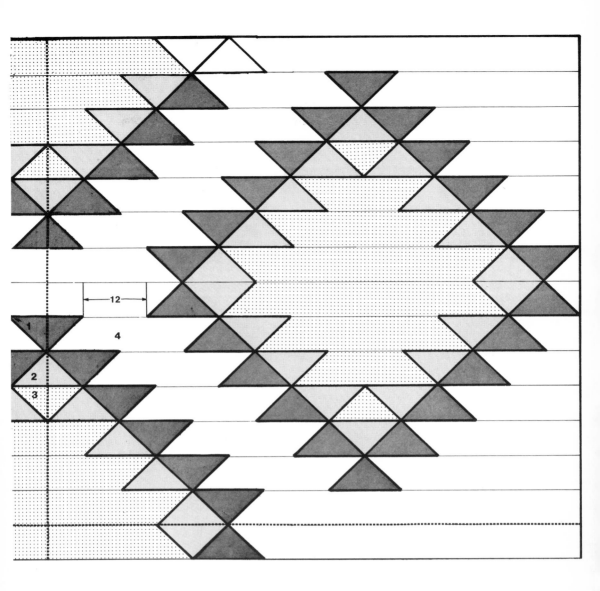

1. black 4

2. 7459 brown 4

3. 7275 gray 5

4. ecru 9

Bring yarn up at arrow. After working first black triangle, work row of black triangles to make diamond-shaped frame for middle section. Work brown triangles, then gray interior. A twelve-stitch section is shown to help you get the correct background spacing. After you have determined the correct location of the second large diamond-shaped section, work the black triangles that make up the frame. Work the ecru background after all the large diamond shapes are completed. This design is 13" wide. If you are using half widths of the D.M.C. 27" canvas, cut a length of 15" and turn it sideways.

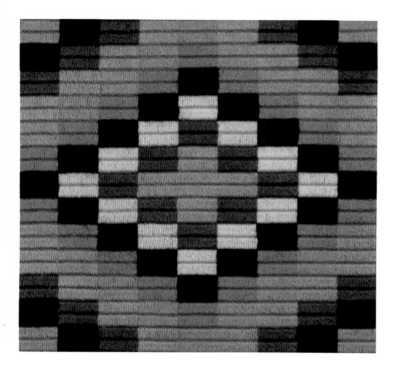

24~

TERRACED
DESIGN

Navaho rug, 1850-75

about 11½″ x 12″

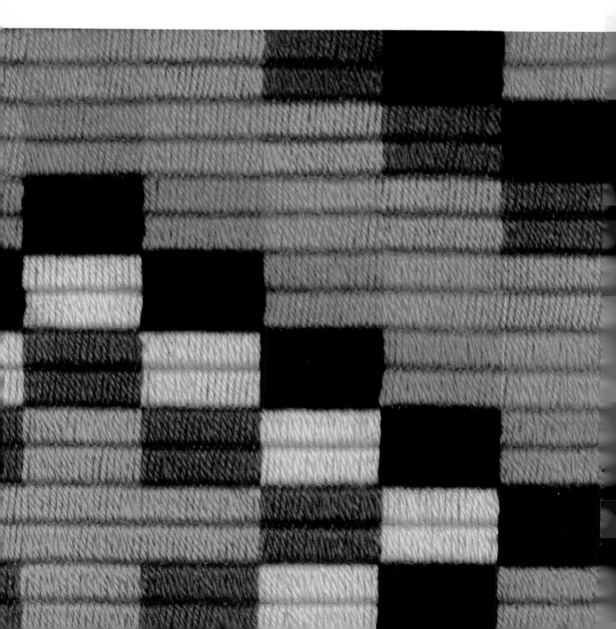

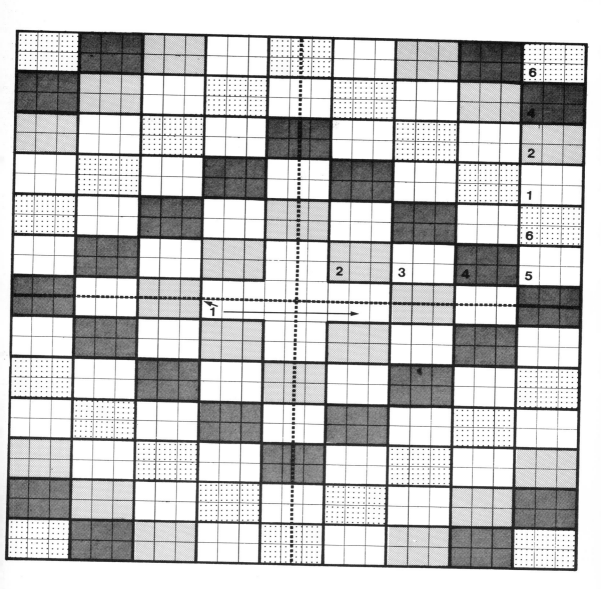

1. 7271 light gray 3
2. 7275 dark gray 3
3. ecru 2

4. black 3
5. 7444 orange 3
6. 7506 gold 3

Bring yarn up at arrow. Work light gray across. Next work the dark gray blocks that surround the central cross. Work each frame of color blocks.

69

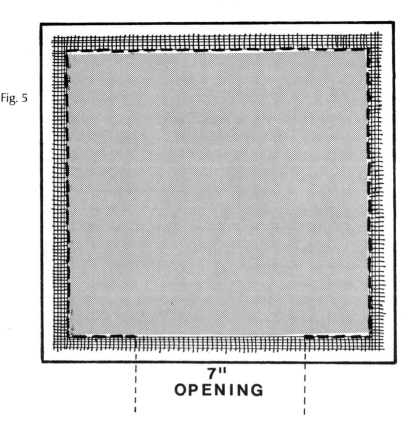

Fig. 5

7"
OPENING

PILLOWS

Sewing the bargello pieces is not difficult if you follow these instructions. Use a fairly heavy material to back the pillows: denim, duck, sailcloth, and various upholstery fabrics work well. My favorite material for backing is heavy natural tan pure linen artist's canvas.

Cut the fabric backing the same size as the bargello piece or a little larger. Place good sides together and pin. Baste by hand, then sew on a machine using a large stitch. If you do not have a machine, sew by hand with small stitches. Sew as close to the yarn as you can, or try stitching a little into the yarn. Try both ways for an inch or so to see which effect you like better. Sometimes it helps to loosen both the top and bottom tensions on the machine. Sew around all four edges leaving about 7" open at the bottom. Before turning good side out, fold and sew the corners as shown in photos—this is the secret of great-looking corners. Then turn good side out and stuff directly with Dacron fiberfil. Pin and hand-stitch bottom opening.

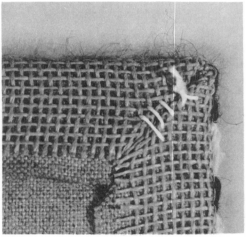

PLATE 25

LARGER PILLOWS

By using borders you can make pillows any size to cover odd-sized cushions you may have. Any heavy fabric will do; real suede and suede cloth were used for the pillows shown. Use masking tape to hold leather or suede in place instead of pinning and basting. A sewing machine with a regular needle will usually work for garment-weight suede and leather. Use a long stitch. It may help to loosen both top and bottom tensions.

Cut two strips the same length as the bargello canvas and two longer strips the width of the canvas plus the width of both strips. Allow several extra inches for seams. Attach shorter strips to side edges of bargello piece, putting good sides together as shown in figure 6; pin, baste, then sew. Always have bargello piece on top so you can stitch along yarn edge. Turn and attach long top and bottom borders next as shown in figure 7. Back pillow and stuff.

Fig. 6

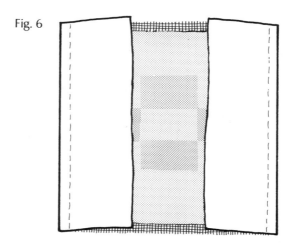

Fig. 7

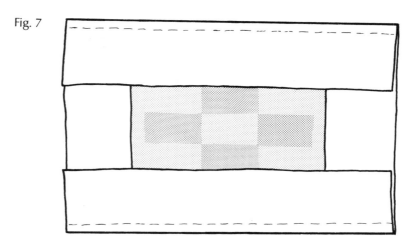

PLATE 26

BAGS

Choose any portion of any design you like to make a bag—full size, middle section, quarter, or less. Heavy fabrics such as denim, sailcloth, linen artist's canvas, and upholstery make good backs. Make your bargello piece whatever size you choose, allowing a border of about 1" all around the edge. Cut fabric back the same size as the piece or a little larger. Pin, baste, and machine stitch three sides leaving the top open. Fold and sew the corners as shown on page 70. This gives the best-looking corners. While the bag is inside out, turn down the top hem and stitch by hand. For the lining use a lighter fabric to make another bag which will fit inside. If you want a zipper in the top of the bag, sew the zipper to the lining before you sew the lining sides together. Keep the lining bag turned inside out so that the good side will be on the inside.

The small bag with the flap was made by cutting the suede back extra long. The excess hangs over the front as a flap. Garment-weight suede and leather combine very well with bargello. When sewing leather, hold in place with masking tape instead of pinning and basting. A regular sewing machine with an ordinary needle usually works fine. Sometimes it helps to loosen both the top and bottom tensions.

Woven cotton strap belts make good handles for large bags. Buy the largest size you can find. Grosgrain ribbon, strips of suede, and leather work well for small bags.

PLATE 27

PHOTO ALBUM (Pineapple Design)

This idea was based on upholstered Victorian photo albums. Use any design; many will come out just the right size to cover an inexpensive standard album. The technique may also be used to cover looseleaf notebooks. The square bargello piece will cover the front and extend a bit around the back. If your piece is not exactly the right height, simply add a border or decrease stitch rows. Cut about a 15″ square of heavy fabric for the back cover of the album. Place good sides together and sew this to the left side of the bargello piece. Fit the resulting fabric and bargello strip around the album. Fold the edges of the bargello piece around the front cover and use bits of tape to hold in place. Fit the corners of the bargello piece around the front cover in the way shown on page 70. Tape the edges securely and evenly in place to the inside of the front cover. Mystic tape can be used to hold it in place permanently. Cut a rectangle of felt to fit the inside cover and glue this down to hide the tape. Fit the fabric on the back cover in the same way, closing the book to make sure the cover fits well. If it ever needs cleaning, use an upholstery or rug cleaner.

Ideas—Use the "Baby Block" pattern in pastel colors for a baby album or use the "Maple Tree" or "Pine Tree" for a family tree album. "Trip around the World" could be used for a travel album or "Diamond" (variation) could be done in the bride's favorite colors for a wedding album.

LOOSELEAF RING NOTEBOOK OR SCRAP-BOOK (Poppy Design)

This is made with a separate back and front connected by snap-open rings.

Cut two pieces of corrugated cardboard, Masonite, or thin plywood to fit bargello piece. Corrugated is most easily cut with an X-acto knife along a metal straightedge.

Within this looseleaf ring sandwich cover, you may put scrapbook refill pages, photo holders, notebook paper, and so on. Use two or three looseleaf metal rings. Make holes in the cardboard or wood at the proper location for the page holes. Fit bargello piece around corners in the way shown on page 70. Tape all edges securely and evenly to inside of cover with Mystik tape. Glue large square of felt to inside of cover to hide the tape. Use a piece of fabric to cover the back of the book in the same way. Ease the metal rings between the bargello stitches and through a canvas space at the hole locations. Cut holes through the felt lining.

76

PLATE 28

ADDRESS BOOK SLIPCOVERS (Section of Double Weave Design)

Make a bargello piece large enough to bend around a closed book. Use any sections you like from any of the designs for these. Cut two fabric pieces large enough to use as linings. Place bargello piece around book inside out. Put linings inside front and back covers and pin in place. Notice how lining is folded so raw edges do not show. When sewing, have bargello piece on top so you can stitch along yarn edges. Keep cover loose enough to allow for bulk of seam when piece is turned right side out. Slip off, baste, then sew by machine. Covers of very small books may need to be steamed with an iron to help them stay closed.

Fig. 8

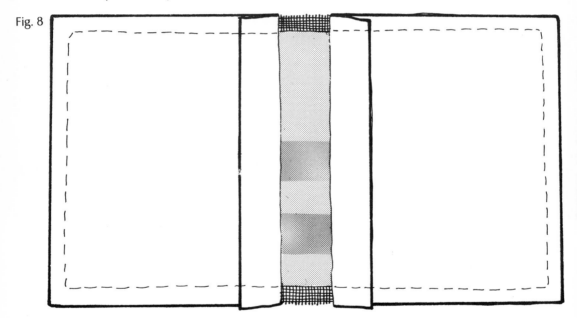

(Section of Log Cabin Design)

Place bargello piece at intended location on front of book. Make two fabric strips the same width as the bargello canvas and large enough to extend over top and bottom of book front, allowing for seams. Placing good sides together, sew these strips to the top and bottom of the bargello piece. Next make a strip 2" wider than the height of the book and long enough to attach to the right side of the bargello piece and go around to cover the entire inside of the front cover. Make another strip the same width, this time long enough to go from the left side of the bargello piece all around the back of the book and to cover the entire inside back cover. Sew these to the bargello piece which already has its top and bottom borders. Fit strip on the book inside out. With book closed, pin in place along top and bottom edges loosely enough to allow for bulk of seam when it is turned. Baste, then sew by machine.

These Address Book Slipcovers are shown in Plate 28.

PLATE 29

FRAMED HANGINGS

Fabric frames are an attractive alternative to ordinary purchased ones. Bargello pieces may also be mounted plain as was the "Sampler." Hanging a piece on a diagonal can give it an entirely different look.

Almost any weight or type of fabric can be used. If your fabric is too transparent, just double it. This was done with the cotton voile print used to frame the "Maple Tree." Ultrasuede was used for the "Pine Tree."

Sew the frame borders following the method on page 72. Be sure to make them wide enough to allow several inches to turn around the back. Trim fabric seams close if necessary to avoid bulk but do not cut or trim canvas.

After you have decided how wide to make frame, cut the backing square to size. Regular brown corrugated cardboard, Masonite, or thin plywood will work. The author used corrugated, cutting with an X-acto knife and metal straight edge.

Center the piece, then tape the bargello canvas edge evenly to the backing square. Next tape the fabric frame to the back of the backing square. You may use bits of tape to "baste" in place, then use strips of wide Mystic tape to attach permanently.

For plain pieces without frames and for frames wider than about ¾", fold and turn the corners as shown on page 70. For thin frames under ¾", a straight right angle fold usually works better; when doing this, fold the top and bottom edges, then the sides.